Brontosaurus

Written by Angela Sheehan
Illustrated by Colin Newman

Library of Congress Cataloging in Publication Data

Sheehan, Angela.
  Brontosaurus.

  Includes index.
  SUMMARY: Follows the path of a young brontosaurus over several days as he forages for leaves, mates, avoids a flesh-eating allosaurus, and escapes from a forest fire.
  1. Brontosaurus—Juvenile literature.   [1. Bronto-saurus.   2. Dinosaurs]   I. Newman, Colin.   II. Title.
QE862.D5S44   1981   567.9'7   81-203
ISBN 0-86592-111-3   AACR1

Ray Rourke Publishing Company, Inc.,
Vero Beach, FL 32964

Brontosaurus
(Apatosaurus)

Pteranodon

Cetiosaurus

Dimetrodon

Iguanodon

Stegosaurus

Brontosaurus

Tyrannosaurus

Triceratops

Parasaurolophus

Ornithomimus

Ankylosaurus

The river was almost dry. There was barely enough water left to cover the crocodiles. Even the spiky horsetails that used to grow thick and fast along the water's edge, were brown and wilted. For days and days there had been no rain.

The young Brontosaurus wallowed in the mud. There was not even enough fresh water to quench his thirst, but the mud cooled his hide. After a while he heaved his great body out of the murky stream and clambered up the bank. The mud caked on his skin dried hard in the baking sun.

The huge animal lumbered off to catch up with his herd. He could hear them bellowing in a maidenhair grove not far off. By the time he reached them the trees were almost bare. The hungry animals had eaten every leaf. Brontosaurus chewed the hard stems, hardly tasting their sap. Soon the sun would go down and the herd would sleep in the grove.

Brontosaurus was too hungry to sleep through the night. He woke often and listened to the calls of the prowling meat-eaters and the screeches of the pterosaurs.

In the morning, the brontosaur herd moved on. They passed a herd of stegosaurs cropping the remains of ferns that not long before had been green and fresh. Now the land was hard and dusty. The scanty patches of plants were almost as brown as the dry soil.

The sun rose high and the herd moved more slowly. They came to a waterhole where they often rested at midday. But it was dry. The trees around it were scorched and wilting. Once more the animals ate what little they could find, then moved on.

As they walked, they passed the skeleton of a dinosaur that had died in the drought. The scavenger Ornitholestes picked the last of the thin flesh from its bones. The brontosaurs picked the last of the leaves from the nearby trees and continued on their way.

Slowly the older animals in the herd began to lag behind. With so little food, they were too tired to walk. The young Brontosaurus also lagged behind, but not because he was weak.

One of the females in the herd was ready to mate. She moved more and more slowly, allowing the others to get far ahead. Only the young male stayed behind with her. The two animals walked side by side. The male roared gently at the female and rubbed her neck with his own. Then after a while they mated.

The sun was sinking now and the two animals were far from the herd. So they found a sheltered spot where there was just enough greenery for them to eat. Then they went to sleep.

The next morning Brontosaurus and his mate hurried after the others. They moved as fast as they could towards the forest. When they were almost within reach of the trees, they heard a frightful roar and a bellowing noise.

Standing as still as they could, they watched an Allosaurus bearing down on one of the old males from their herd. In his youth no Allosaurus would have been a match for him. But now the animal was too old and weak, and the great flesh-eater was savage with hunger. Brontosaurus and his mate saw its claws rip through the old animal's hide and its rasping teeth dig deep into the wound. With a bellow of pain, the old dinosaur sank dead to the ground. Allosaurus gorged. Now it was safe for the two younger animals to pass by.

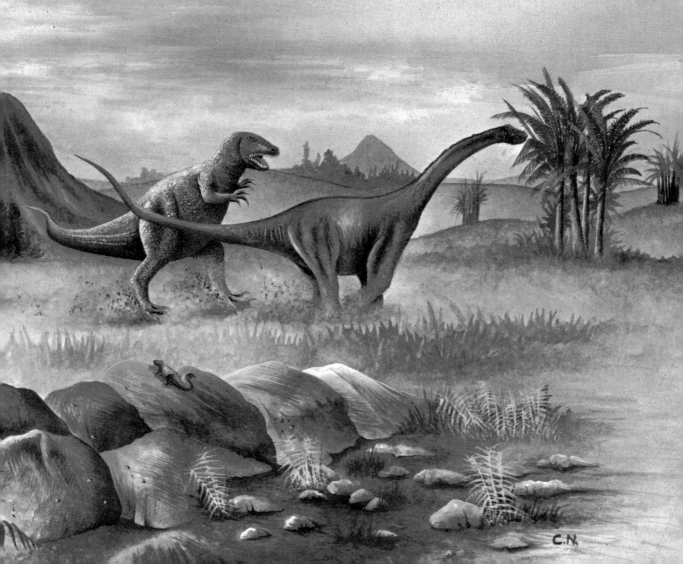

By the time Brontosaurus and his mate reached
the forest, the others had moved into its depths,
munching the leaves as they went. The two animals
ate and ate and ate as they followed them. For the
first time in days they had enough to eat, and the
trees sheltered them from the sun. They lazed for a
while in the shade and then moved on. Ahead of them
they could hear the bellows of the well-fed herd. By
nightfall they had almost caught up with them.

Then suddenly out of the sky came a great
flash of light and a mighty rumble. All the animals
bellowed and roared in terror. The birds took to flight
and the dinosaurs ran. The two brontosaurs charged
through the trees, crashing against the trunks and
trampling the dry undergrowth. When they stopped,
there was silence. The silence lasted a few moments.
Then the dreadful light and sound came again,
followed once more by stillness.

The two animals waited. After a while they heard a new sound, crackling and roaring. The wind carried a strange, frightening smell. All the animals were on the move. Huge flesh-eaters headed the charge, followed by small nimble dinosaurs and scampering mammals. Lizards darted from their hiding places and pterosaurs took to the air. Brontosaurus and his mate galloped along with the others in their panic.

The whole forest was on fire. Flames and sparks, fanned by the wind, leapt from the burning branches. The animals ran and ran and ran. The flames licked along behind them, eating up the ferns and the cycads. Smoke blocked out the light of the moon. The forest was lit only by the giant red flames.

Brontosaurus and his mate ran until they could almost run no more. At last they came to an outcrop of bare rock. They scrambled up the steep cliff face, joining the other animals that had fled there from the fire. They clambered from ledge to ledge, not knowing where to go.

But the blaze could not reach them. The rocks were bare. There was nothing to burn. So they were safe. All night the fire raged below them. They watched and waited.

By morning there was nothing left of the forest but bare, blackened tree trunks standing in a layer of ash. The animals picked their way down the cliffs to the level ground, and went on their way.

As they lumbered over the rocks, Brontosaurus and his mate came upon the rest of their herd. They too had fled from the fire, but they were all safe. Together now, they moved across the plain, searching for trees to eat, as the other animals searched for ferns on the ground, or hunted their prey.

Brontosaurus soon grew hot and tired again. There were no trees, and the only pool they found was almost dry. By evening they had still found nothing to eat or drink.

Then suddenly the same light flashed that had
flashed the night before and the same rumbling
followed. But this time, instead of fire, the animals felt
soft, cool drops of water on their hides. The clouds
opened and rain poured from the sky. Great drops
splashed on to the ground and soon rivers of water
roared among the stones. Within minutes the empty
waterhole was filled. Brontosaurus and his mate
trampled in the pool and sucked up the cool water.

From then on it rained every day. The dusty ground sprang to life. Ranks of ferns grew up and the trees sprouted new leaves. The land grew green almost overnight. The brontosaur herd was able to stay where it was.

Brontosaurus spent each new day trundling
about munching first one tree, then another. His mate,
too, ate well. Later in the year she laid her eggs. And
before the dry season came again young brontosaurs
hatched from the eggs.

Brontosaurus and the Jurassic World

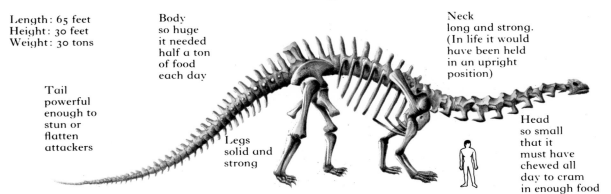

Length: 65 feet
Height: 30 feet
Weight: 30 tons

Body so huge it needed half a ton of food each day

Neck long and strong. (In life it would have been held in an upright position)

Tail powerful enough to stun or flatten attackers

Legs solid and strong

Head so small that it must have chewed all day to cram in enough food

The skeleton of Brontosaurus compared in size with a man

"Thunder Lizard"

The name Brontosaurus means "thunder lizard". Imagine the noise a herd of them would have made as they trundled along, and you will realize what a good name it is. Brontosaurus is also now called Apatosaurus.

Brontosaurus was one of the largest animals ever to live. It belonged to a group of plant-eating dinosaurs, called sauropods. There were lots of different kinds, but they were all huge (see opposite page). Diplodocus was longer than Brontosaurus; Brachiosaurus was bigger and heavier. He must have weighed as much as 100 tons. Unlike the other sauropods, his front legs were larger than the back ones.

When did Brontosaurus live?

Brontosaurus lived 150 million years ago during the Jurassic period. This was the middle period of the Age of Dinosaurs. The earlier period is called the Triassic and the one following it the Cretaceous.

Plants of the Jurassic

During the Jurassic, the climate was warm, and the earth was covered with dense growths of ferns and other plants for the dinosaurs to eat. Palm-like cycads with thick trunks and huge leaves grew everywhere. There were conifer trees, such as pines and redwoods, and there were lots of maidenhair, or ginkgo, trees. They were the chief food for the brontosaurs—you can see their fan-shaped leaves on page 9.

Animals of the Jurassic

Many fierce flesh-eating dinosaurs lived at the same time as Brontosaurus. The largest was Allosaurus (see page 11), a ferocious monster that strode about on its huge back legs. The adult sauropods were probably safe from the meat-eaters. Like elephants today, they were just too big to be attacked. But the younger brontosaurs and old, weak ones were probably easy prey. A smaller plant-eater, such as Stegosaurus (see pages 6 & 16) would also have given Allosaurus little trouble.

Small meat-eaters would never have tackled the armored plant-eaters or the sauropods. They probably fed on dead animals (as Ornitholestes is doing on page 7), or on the remains of the kills of the larger dinosaurs. They may also have trailed the herds of plant-eaters to pick up small lizards and insects disturbed by the dinosaurs' feet.

Land Lovers

People once thought that the sauropods lived in lakes, with water to support their great weight. But today scientists think that they must have lived on land, using their long necks to browse on the treetops, as giraffes do. A 40-foot-long neck would have had no use in the water. If the animal had gone into deep water and tried to breathe with its nose at the surface, it would have been unable to do so: the weight of the water on its chest would have been too great for it to breathe in.

Living Together

Most of the big plant-eating animals that live today move about in herds. Elephants, antelopes, giraffes and kangaroos all travel and feed together. The herd gives them protection. A lion is far more likely to attack a lone animal than a whole herd. Also animals can warn each other of danger. The same thing probably happened in prehistoric times. We know for certain that Iguanodon, a Cretaceous dinosaur, lived in herds. The bones of twenty of them were found all in one place in Belgium. They probably died in a landslide.

Brontosaurus and the other plant-eating dinosaurs probably also formed herds, though the brontosaur herds could not have been very large. Just one Brontosaurus would have eaten about 1000 pounds of food every day. If very many of them had traveled together, there would have been no plants left.

Brontosaur Babies

As far as we know, all dinosaurs laid eggs. Newly hatched Brontosaurs would have been no more than about a yard long. They would have been too small to travel with a herd, even if their parents' herd had stayed in the place where the eggs were laid. So the young probably spent their early lives hidden among the ferns. As they grew, they would have joined up with other youngsters for safety's sake. If, by chance, their parents' herd had still been in the same area when they were ready to travel, they might have joined their herd. The youngster on page 20 of the story is just big enough to wander with his parents' herd. But it is more likely that he would have stayed a little longer with his brothers and sisters while his parents moved on.

Brontosaurus compared with some other sauropods: Diplodocus was the longest, Brachiosaurus the biggest

Picture Index

Apart from Brontosaurus, these are some of the other animals that you can see in the book:

Things To Do

Try to think of animals living today that are like the dinosaurs in the story. Brontosaurus was like an elephant or a giraffe. What modern animal do you think Allosaurus is like?

Nobody has ever seen a dinosaur. So we can only guess what they looked like from their skeletons. The artist has drawn Brontosaurus the same color as an elephant. You draw him the color you think he might have been.

Make models of some of the animals in the book with modeling clay. Then paint them and put them into a scene, using paper for the ferns and trees.

Melanorosaurus

Cetiosaurus

Brachiosaurus

Diplodocus

Brontosaurus